START EXPLORING™

FOLKTALES

OF NATIVE AMERICANS

A STORY-FILLED COLORING BOOK

David Borgenicht

Illustrated by Helen I. Driggs

Running Press
Philadelphia, Pennsylvania

Canadian representatives: General Publishing Co., Ltd.,
30 Lesmill Road, Don Mills, Ontario M3B 2T6

International representatives: Worldwide Media Services, Inc.,
30 Montgomery Street, Jersey City, New Jersey 07302

9 8 7 6 5 4 3 2 1
Digit on the right indicates the number of this printing.

ISBN 1–56138–303–1

Editorial Director: Nancy Steele
Cover design: E. June Roberts
Interior design: Lili Schwartz
Cover, interior, and poster illustrations: Helen I. Driggs
Poster copyright © 1993 Running Press Book Publishers
Typography: Garamond & Xavier by Richard Conklin
Printed by Banta Corporation

This book may be ordered by mail from the publisher.
Please add $2.50 for postage and handling.
But try your bookstore first!

Running Press Book Publishers
125 South Twenty-second Street
Philadelphia, Pennsylvania 19103–4399

CONTENTS

Native American Peoples: An Introduction

Each group of Native Americans has a unique heritage of myths and folklore. These are the peoples whose stories are told here.

Assiniboine—A group of Indians who now live in Montana and southwest Canada. They were originally members of the Yanktonnai nation of Dakota Sioux.

Brule Sioux—A large group of the Dakota Sioux, now living in South Dakota and Nebraska.

Cherokee—The largest numbers of these Native Americans are now in Oklahoma, but the Cherokee people once lived throughout the region around North Carolina and northern Georgia. Their language is Iroquois.

Chippewa—A group of Indians who lived in what is now Michigan, around Lake Superior. They also are known as the Ojibwa.

Cochiti—A group of pueblo Indians who live in the southwestern United States, along the Rio Grande.

Crow—A group of western Plains Indians who lived in what is now Wyoming and Montana.

Dakota—The largest group of the Sioux Indians, located in the midwestern United States.

Menomini—A group of Indians who lived in upper Michigan and Wisconsin. Their customs were similar to those of the Chippewa.

Papago—A southwestern nation whose members made their homes at the bases of canyons in what is now Arizona and New Mexico.

Seneca—A group of Indians from the northeastern United States, near New York, and the Midwest, around Lake Erie.

Sioux—A large group of Indians from the Midwest, divided into three distinct groups: Lakota, Dakota, and Nakota.

Tête de Boule—A group of Indians who were members of the Algonquin people. They were located in Canada, in the area of Quebec.

Tewa—A group of pueblo Indians from the southwestern United States, now New Mexico.

Tsimshian—A group of Indians located on the northwest coast of North America, along Canada's shoreline between British Columbia and Alaska.

INTRODUCTION

These tales have been told before.

No one really knows how many times—only in the last hundred years have they even been written down. Before that, they were only spoken. Around a campfire, within a lodge, after a great feast, these stories and thousands more were passed on from father to son, from sister to brother, from person to person—by voice alone. Today, on reservations and among Native American families throughout the country, that oral tradition continues.

In the late 19th and early 20th centuries, scholars began to record Native American stories. They visited many Native American nations to gather the legends and translate them. Often they heard several versions of the same tale within one nation. Sometimes, because the Native Americans were fearful of giving away their culture to outsiders, they changed the stories they told. But by collecting the different versions of each tale and comparing them, authentic versions could be constructed.

The words may have changed over the centuries, but the essence of these stories has not. Here are tales of warriors, tricksters, giants, coyotes, butterflies, and ghosts. Here, seasons change, animals race, and worlds are created. Within these pages live the beliefs, history, and personalities of the peoples who originated them long ago and who still tell them today.

Now you can be a part of the tradition. Read, color, and imagine these stories, and pass them along.

WALKS-ACROSS-THE-SKY

A Tsimshian Story

In the beginning, before all living things were created, the chief of a great tribe lived in the sky with his two sons and a daughter. The world around them was empty and dark.

The young son, called One-Who-Walks-Across-the-Sky, was tired of all the darkness. While he was chopping wood, he had an idea how to make the world light. He took a long, slender cedar branch and bent it into a ring, just larger than his face. Then, he tied firewood all around the ring, so that it looked like a large round mask, with a great wide smile.

One-Who-Walks-Across-the-Sky then set the mask on fire and put it on. With his face blazing, he ran across the heavens from east to west, moving quickly so that the mask would not scorch him.

Everyone in the land of the sky saw the great light come up and move quickly to the west. The people were very happy to have light, even for only a few minutes. So the young son did this every day— and this was how the sun came to be.

Sometimes, when people have a little of something, even though they had nothing before, they soon want more. So one day the tribe called a council with the chief, and told him that they wanted his son to slow down.

"We want more light," the people complained. But the young son, who was taking part in the council, said that he could not go slower.

"If I do not move quickly, the mask will burn up before I reach the west, and my face will be burned," he explained. The people accepted his answer, but they walked away grumbling. After the council had met, the boy's little sister, Support-of-Sun, whispered to her father.

"I'll try to hold him back a little tomorrow, so that the people can have more light," she said.

The next day, One-Who-Walks-Across-the-Sky rose in the east, as he always had. But when he began his rapid journey, his sister ran after him, calling, "Wait for me! Wait for me!"

Her brother paused in the middle of the sky to wait for his sister, and when she had caught up, she kept him busy talking for a while. This is why the sun stops and hovers mid-sky at noon. The boy's mask did not burn up, and the people were happy.

Meanwhile, the older son, Walking-About-Early, was not happy letting his younger brother have all the attention. Also, his father was pressuring him to do something good for the world. He decided that he too would run across the sky—but just after midnight, when it was still dark.

Walking-About-Early

The Months

In this legend, the animals hold a council to decide the length of days, months, and years. They also name some of the months.

These are the names that the Tsimshian people gave to the months of the year:

January — Spring Salmon Month

February — Month When Olachen (or eulachon, a fish) is Eaten

March and April — Month When Olachen is Cooked

May — Egg Month

June — Salmon Month

July and August — Humpback Salmon Month

September — Spinning Top Month (a time to carve wooden tops used to play games of chance during the winter months)

October — Falling Leaf Month

November — Taboo Month (a time for preparation for a season of hunting and fishing, when the Tsimshian people fasted and drank sacred drinks for good luck; breaking this tradition was forbidden, or taboo)

December — In-between Month

rubbed fat and charcoal all over his face, and as he crossed the night sky, his face reflected light from the night fires. But this light was a dull, soothing light, unlike the light from his brother's mask.

The people saw him, and were glad to see a glowing face rising in the night sky. In this way, Walking-About-Early became the moon.

Much time passed, with the sun rising and setting every day, and the moon coming and going every night. Animals were created to live on the world below, and they held a council.

They decided that it was good for the sun to rise during the day and the moon to rise at night. But they could not decide how many days and nights this should happen every month.

The dogs spoke first. "The moon should grow for 20 days, and then shrink for 20 days. The months will be 40 days long." There was a large grumble in the council. Most animals did not like this idea.

The porcupine tapped the head dog on the shoulder.

"Ow!" the dog exclaimed. "What is it?" He plucked a quill from his back.

"With 40 days a month, the year would be too long. There should only be 30 days in a month," said the porcupine.

There was large applause from the council. Everyone but the dogs agreed. So it was decided that each month would have 30 days, and each year 12 months. The dogs were so angry with the porcupine and the rest of the animals for ignoring their suggestion that they never forgave the forest creatures. This is why dogs and creatures of the woods do not get along.

Up in the sky, new things were happening. Walks-Across-the-Sky took to wearing his mask to bed. He snored terribly, and while he slept and snored, sparks from his mask blew off and scattered into the night. They settled there, and became the stars.

Walks-Across-the-Sky also took to painting his face with his sister's red paint when he was happy. This told people what the weather would be like—if the sun was red in the evening, then the weather would be good the next day. If it was red in the morning, storms would be coming.

Their father praised Walks-Across-the-Sky and Walking-About-Early for their role in creation, but he scolded Support-of-Sun for the small part she had played. She wandered sadly into the west, and into the great waters there. When she returned, completely wet, she stood by her father's blazing fire and wrung out her clothes.

Accidentally, Support-of-Sun dripped water into the flames, and a great cloud of steam floated out over the world. This created a damp fog which helped cool the hot days. Finally, the chief was pleased with her.

In this way, all the chief's children helped to make the world.

OLD MAN COYOTE MAKES THE WORLD

A Crow Story

Nobody knows where the water came from. Nobody knows where Old Man Coyote came from, either. But in the beginning, there he was—and all that existed around him was the water.

"It is bad that I am alone," he said to no one but the waves. "I should have someone to speak with." So Old Man Coyote began to look around for a friend. No one and nothing could be seen. He was sure that he was alone in the world—until he came upon two ducks with red eyes.

"Brothers!" he said, excited to see other creatures, "Is there anything in this world but water and more water? Tell me what you have seen."

"Well," began the ducks, "we have seen nothing. But we think that there might be something *below* the water."

Old Man Coyote was happy with that thought. "Please, younger brothers, will you go down and find out? Dive down and see if there is something. Go!"

With that, one of the ducks dived. He stayed down for a long time. Old Man Coyote waited and waited. Nothing. He looked over the edge of the water, and spoke.

"How sad," Coyote said. "Our younger brother must have drowned."

But the other duck was not afraid. "No, he has not drowned. We ducks can live underwater for a long time. Be patient."

Again, they waited. At last the first duck surfaced.

"There is something below!" he said to his brothers. "I bumped into it with my head!"

They were all excited now. "Well, bring it up, younger brother, bring it up!" said Old Man Coyote. And the duck dived again.

This time, he stayed down even longer. Old Man Coyote was worried, and just about to say so, when the duck came up. He had something in his beak.

"What is that?" asked the coyote. He took the thing from the duck's mouth, and looked hard at it. "Why, it's a root," he said. "And where there are roots, there must be soil. Younger brother, dive down again—and if you find something soft and brown near where the root was, bring it up."

For a third time the duck went down. He stayed under longer than the first and second dives together. But when he came up, he had a small lump of soft earth in his beak. Old Man Coyote took it in his hands.

"This is what I wanted, younger brother!" he said excitedly. "I will make this grow, and spread it around. In my hand, out of this little ball of mud, I will make our home."

And with that, Old Man Coyote blew hard on the lump. It began to grow. It became too large for his hand, and fell into the water. But instead of sinking, it spread all over and formed a huge mass of land.

Then, Old Man Coyote took the root and planted it in the soft earth. Almost immediately, grasses, plants, trees, and flowers started to

grow. Fruit trees appeared, food was all around. Old Man Coyote was very pleased.

"Look at how beautiful this is," he said. "What do you think?"

But the ducks were not as pleased. "It looks wonderful, elder brother—but it's too flat. Why don't you shape it? Make some places wider, and add some big mounds for hills and mountains."

Old Man Coyote thought for a moment, and then looked out at the land. "Yes, my younger brothers," he said, "I will do as you say. And I will even make some trails for the water to follow so that wherever we go, we will have good water to drink."

"Thank you, elder brother," said the ducks. When Old Man Coyote had finished making the mountains and the streams, the ducks told him how clever he was. But Old Man Coyote looked unhappy.

"Something is still missing," he said. "What do you think it is?"

The ducks thought that everything looked beautiful, and had no idea what could be wrong. But Old Man Coyote knew.

"Friends are missing," he said. "We have each other, but it will be dull with no one else."

So he took up another ball of mud, and made men. Just how he did this, no one knows. But there they were, walking around and learning to live.

The Crow Indians

The Crow Indians of the western Plains—in what is now Wyoming and Montana, near the Yellowstone River and the eastern side of the Rocky Mountains—were nomadic. They lived in tipis, and moved camp often.

Old Man Coyote watched them, and was very pleased with his creation. This time, however, the ducks looked unhappy.

"What is wrong, my younger brothers?" he asked them.

"You have made companions for yourself—but there is still no one for us," they answered.

Old Man Coyote felt stupid. He slapped his head in forgetfulness.

"I forgot!" he exclaimed. And right away he made all kinds of ducks. "Now you can be happy again."

They all watched the new life. After some time, Old Man Coyote looked puzzled again.

"Something is still not right," he said.

The ducks replied, "But everything is beautiful. We have food, water, companions—what could be missing?"

Then, Old Man Coyote knew. He slapped his head again. "Don't you see? All of these people are male, and all of these ducks are male! How can they be happy and increase?"

With that, he made women—and female ducks. And with that, there was happiness, and the world grew. That is how it began.

The Crow people were once linked to a more settled tribe, the Hidatsa, but the two groups separated around 1650.

The Crow often fought with Dakota and Siksika Indians. During the winter months, tales such as this were told—it was considered unlucky to tell stories in the summer, when there was so much that needed to be done.

HOW THE ANIMALS WERE CREATED

A Crow Story

After he had created the world and all that lived in it, Old Man Coyote walked about to see what he had made. Suddenly, he came upon another coyote! The old coyote was surprised to see something he hadn't made, but he was happy to meet him.

"My younger brother!" he said to the coyote. "What a surprise! How did you get here?"

Sounding confused, the coyote spoke. "I do not know, my elder brother. I do not know where I came from, or how I came to this place. All I know is that I am on the earth, and happy to be here. I call myself Cirape."

Old Man Coyote introduced himself, and waved his arm wide. "All that you see around you, I have made." He was very proud.

Cirape looked long and hard at the world. "You did a good job," he said. "But—" he paused.

Now Old Man Coyote was confused. "But what, younger brother?"

"Well," Cirape replied, "the people and ducks are all very well— but don't you think that there should be some other animals?"

Old Man Coyote agreed right away. "You're right. When I say the names of the animals, they will appear." Old Man Coyote called

out: buffalo, elk, deer, antelope, and bear. And they all appeared. He made all kinds of small animals, too.

The bear noticed the coyotes, and came over to them. He sat next to Old Man Coyote.

"Thank you for making me, brother," he said, "but what am I supposed to do here?"

Old Man Coyote didn't understand. "I have made all kinds of friends for you. Isn't that enough?"

"But we have nothing to do."

"True," said Old Man Coyote. "I'll think of something." And he did. "I'll make a special bird!"

He took one of the bear's claws and made wings from it. How, we do not know. But he did it. He took caterpillar hair and made feet. From a buffalo muscle he made a beak. From leaves, he created a tail. Putting all these things together, he made a prairie chicken.

But the old coyote was not done. "There are many beautiful birds," he said to the new creature. "But you I will not make beautiful. I will give you a special power. Every day, when the sun comes up, you will dance for the new day. You will hop and strut. You will raise your tail. You will shake and spread your wings, and you will dance—like this!" And he waved his arm.

The prairie chicken danced, and as all the other animals watched, they began to dance too. Now, they had something to do!

But the bear still was not pleased. "I give my claw so that you can make a prairie chicken," he said, "and you give him a dance! Why don't you give me a dance?"

Old Man Coyote only wanted to make the creatures in the world happy. "All right," he said. "But I will give you your own dance." He waved his arm. "There, now you have a dance."

But the bear did not feel like dancing. "How can I dance? Something is missing."

"What could be missing?" Old Man Coyote asked. "I have made everything everyone has asked for!"

"A sound," the bear answered. "We must have some kind of sound to dance to."

"Dance to the sound of the world," Old Man Coyote said. But this was not enough for the bear.

And so the old coyote took a grouse that was flying by and gave him a song to sing. Then, he gave the people drums. The grouse sang, and the people drummed, and everyone danced—even the bear.

Still, the bear complained. Old Man Coyote was becoming angry.

"Why should the prairie chicken dance?" the bear asked. "Why should any of these tiny animals dance? I alone should have the power to dance!"

"But they are happy," said the old coyote. "The fruit is ripening, the water is rippling, and the sun is shining. Everyone feels like dancing. Why should you be the only one to dance?"

The bear stood up tall. "I am big. I am strong. I am the most important one. I alone should dance."

Old Man Coyote was amazed. "Look at this one," he said to Cirape, who was busy watching the other animals dance. "Who does he think he is? I made him!"

"Ha!" the bear laughed. "I made myself." He had a short memory. He also had a short temper, and he began swatting at the small animals that danced around him to get them to stop.

"You are very rude," Old Man Coyote said. "You are not fit to live with us. From now on, you will stay in a den by yourself. You will eat decayed things. You will sleep all winter long—the less we see of you, the better."

And so it became.

SCATTERING THE STARS

A Cochiti Story

Long ago, after a great flood had cleared the world, everything began to live again. Flowers sprouted. Trees grew tall once more. Animals came out of hiding. And the Cochiti people came out too, from the north.

The Mother of the Cochiti people guided them in their journey south, back to their land. She told them that all people were brothers and sisters, and to treat all living things with kindness. With this in mind, the tribe started south.

But a little girl was left behind. The Mother saw that they had left her, and called her.

"Kotcimanyako, come here."

When the girl came, the Mother gave her a little bag made of simple, white cotton to carry. She explained to her, "No matter what happens, do not unwrap this bag. It will keep you safe."

"What is in it?" the girl wondered.

"It does not matter," the Mother quickly answered. "All that matters is that it will keep you safe, and that you do not unwrap what is within the bag."

Kotcimanyako promised, and set off to follow her people. But she was still curious.

She walked for a long time, trying to keep her mind off her bundle. She looked at the sky, and the mountains around her. She

looked at the path, and wondered where her people had gone. But she always returned to one thought—she wondered what the bag held.

She could not understand why she was forbidden to peek. *Surely,* she thought, *one peek wouldn't hurt.* She wouldn't even touch whatever the bag was holding!

As the sun began to set, Kotcimanyako sat down for a rest, and placed the bundle on the ground. She noticed that it was tied very tightly, with many knots. One by one, she undid them.

Finally, she came to the last knot, and the bag began to overflow. Tiny specks of light were spilling out of the opening! They flew about her, and she smiled, though she still didn't know what they were.

At first there were just a few pinpoints of light around her—but soon there were hundreds in the air! Kotcimanyako began to be a bit frightened. She tried to catch them in her hands and put them back in her bag, but every time she caught one and put it back in the bag, several more flew out.

The bag began to move, and suddenly it burst open.

Thousands upon thousands of lights flew into the air, and up into

The Cochiti People

The Cochiti people live in New Mexico, in a pueblo along the Rio Grande. Ruins of old Cochiti villages can be seen on a high, flat mountain nearby, the Cochiti Mesa.

Even though this region is dry, the Cochiti have always been a farming people. Most of their traditional ceremonies revolve around solstice.

A familiar part of Cochiti culture is the famous southwest "Storyteller" figure, a sculpture of a woman with as many as a dozen small children sitting on her lap as she tells tales.

the sky. They scattered all over the heavens. The sky had become completely dark now, and the lights seemed to blink on and off in the night sky.

Kotcimanyako had managed to get a few of the lights back into the bag. These lights struggled to get out to be with the others in the sky. But she held the bag tightly closed, and set off again on her journey.

When she had joined her people, she took out the lights one by one, and arranged them carefully in the sky, where we see them now. These are the stars that we know by name—the Slingshot Stars, the Pot-rest Stars, the Shield Stars, and a few more.

And that is why some stars form pictures in the sky, and others do not.

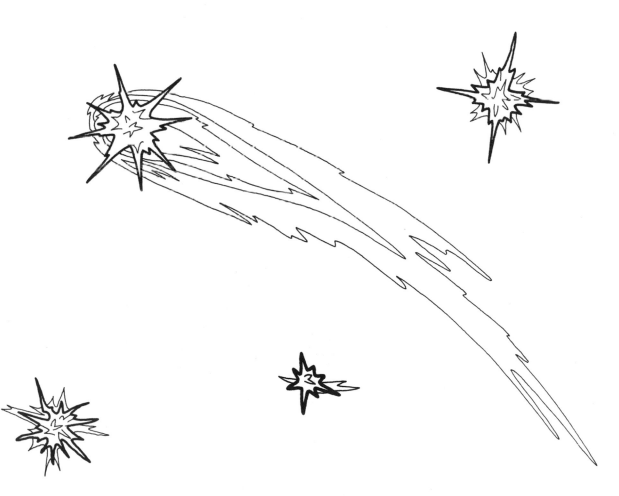

THE FIRST FOLKTALES

A Seneca Story

Once there was a boy named Gaqka whose parents died when he was very young. His relatives would not care for him, and he had no home. He lived in a tiny hut made of fallen branches, and he hunted small animals for food.

Gaqka wore ragged clothes, and rarely washed. The people from his village called him "Filth-Covered-One," and laughed whenever he walked by. They thought he would never make anything of himself.

Gaqka was tired of living such a sad life—being laughed at, having no one to care for him, and living like an animal. So he decided to leave his people, and to become a great hunter.

Late one night, Gaqka walked far into the forest. The sounds of the night frightened him—he had never really left his village before—but he walked on, carrying nothing with him but his pipe, a bow, and some arrows.

The world around him was pitch black. He could not see in front of his face—and this is why he tripped and fell over something in his path. Gaqka brushed himself off, and tried to see what he had run into.

It was a canoe. *How strange*, he thought, *to find a canoe in the middle of a forest with no water nearby.* Gaqka felt around on the ground next to the canoe. Not too far away, he found an oar and picked it up.

Gaqka carried the oar back to the canoe and stepped in. At once the canoe shot up into the air and hovered above the treetops. Needless to say, Gaqka was astonished. But he had been in canoes before, and he knew that to make them move, you had to paddle.

Grasping the oar with both hands, he paddled the air around him. The canoe began to move—slowly at first, and then as fast as the wind! Higher and higher he paddled into the night sky, up beyond the clouds, and just beneath the moon. Then, perhaps because he caught the wind, the canoe drifted back toward Earth. After a long glide, the canoe dropped into a river, and Gaqka paddled toward shore.

When he reached land, Gaqka saw a great cliff not far off that had a face like a man. Taking this to be a sign (although of what he had no idea), Gaqka made his way to the cliff and began climbing. After a long, hard climb, Gaqka reached the top. There he built a hut out of tree bark, and resolved to make this his new home.

Happy with his new life and the adventures he'd already had, Gaqka moved to the edge of the cliff, and sat on a rock there—to smoke his pipe, to think, and to look at the world beyond.

Just as Gaqka was filling his pipe, he heard a voice say, "Give me some tobacco." He looked around. No one was there.

"Where are you?" Gaqka asked. "If I cannot see you, why should I give you tobacco?"

No answer. Gaqka waited a moment longer to see if the voice would respond, but still he heard nothing. He went back to loading his pipe.

After his smoke, Gaqka took out his arrows and began to bind them tighter, preparing for the next day's hunt.

Again, the voice spoke, "Give me some tobacco!" The voice seemed to be coming from over the cliff.

Gaqka was curious now, so he took a pinch of tobacco and threw it out over the cliff, toward where the voice seemed to be coming from.

The voice spoke again. "Thank you. I will now tell you a tale."

Amazed at what was happening, the boy listened to the story. It seemed to echo out directly from the rock on which he was sitting. It was a wonderful story about a great spirit who lived in the air. The boy had never heard this story before. In fact, Gaqka had never heard any story before—nobody ever told stories.

Finally, the story ended. "Now," said the voice from the rock, "it will be the custom for you to give me a gift whenever I tell you one of my stories."

Gaqka gave the rock a few beads of bone, which he was carrying so that he could carve them into arrowheads.

"Thank you again," said the voice.

"You are most welcome," said Gaqka. "I hope to hear your stories often, for this is my home now."

"I would be pleased to tell you my tales whenever you like," said the voice. "But you must promise to give me gifts for them, and never to fall asleep until the tales are over."

"Agreed," said Gaqka, "and since the first tale is now over, I must go rest. Goodnight."

Gaqka went into his hut and slept more peacefully than he ever had before.

The next day, Gaqka hunted well. He killed many birds, and thanked the great father for the good hunt. Then, he made some of the birds into a soup, roasted others, and saved the skins in his bag.

That night, after dinner, the boy sat upon the rock once again and watched the sun sink. He wondered if the voice would speak.

Gaqka took out his knife and some bone bits, and began carving arrowheads. Just as the first arrowhead was done, the voice came.

"Give me some tobacco, friend," it said.

Again Gaqka threw some tobacco over the cliff. "Thank you," said the voice, and began to tell stories. One tale came after another—some of them were exciting, some beautiful, some funny. Gaqka listened to the tales long into the night and was becoming quite tired when the voice called out,

"My stories tonight are finished."

Gaqka was sorry to have the stories end, but he was glad to get some rest. He gave the rock an awl he had made from a bird's leg, another pinch of tobacco, and went to sleep in his hut.

The next day, the boy decided to hunt in the east. He walked far, but birds and animals did not seem to be around. He walked farther. Finally, he came upon a village. There he found friendly people, people much more friendly than those in his own village.

Gaqka met some great hunters who offered to teach him how to hunt big game. He spent the night in the village, and the next day they went off on a hunt together. It was a good day for hunting, but it was a long hunt and they were far from the village. Gaqka decided to take them back to his camp on the high cliff.

They ate well, and talked much of their lives. Then, Gaqka took them over to the edge of the cliff.

"Now," Gaqka said, "we will hear some tales."

"Tales?" one of the hunters asked. "What are they?"

"I will show you," Gaqka said. And he sat upon the rock.

Together, they listened to stories, and were enchanted by the words. In this way, Gaqka made many friends in the new village. People spoke to him with respect, and helped him to find his place and to take care of himself.

Now that he was a respected hunter, Gaqka decided that he wanted a decorated pouch for his arrowheads. He went into the village one day, and after asking for advice about who could make such a pouch, he reached a house at the edge of the village where two daughters lived with their mother.

He knocked, and went inside.

The mother and younger daughter smiled brightly when he entered. The older daughter frowned.

"I am looking for someone to make me a pouch," Gaqka said to the mother.

The younger daughter spoke up. "It is finished," she said. "I have been waiting for you to come for it." From behind her back she brought out a beautiful beaded pouch.

"It is perfect," said Gaqka. "How did you know?" He looked deep into the young woman's eyes. Her older sister snorted in disgust.

"I believe that my future son-in-law has come into our home," said the mother. Gaqka smiled at her, and to the younger daughter. She smiled back.

The young daughter went into the back of the house, and brought out a basket of bread for all to eat.

"My mother wants us to marry," said the young woman as they ate together.

"She is not the only one," said Gaqka.

"Hah!" said the older daughter.

After the meal, and after the mother and older daughter went to sleep, the young woman spoke to Gaqka in a whisper.

"We must leave tonight! My older sister will try to kill you if we do not—she is very jealous of me."

Gaqka understood. He had seen the older daughter's anger. So they arose together, gathered up their belongings, and headed straight to Gaqka's clifftop camp.

"This is where I live," he explained. Then he led her over to the rock. "And this is the storytelling rock." The young woman smiled. She did not look as confused as the hunters had.

"I will show you," Gaqka explained. With that, they sat upon the rock. They heard wonderful tales of what had happened in olden times, before the world had been made. They heard how people came to be, and how the animals learned to get along and to survive. They listened long into the night.

But the young woman was not surprised by a storytelling rock.

"This rock," she explained, "is the spirit of my grandfather. I know his voice. He wants someone to continue to tell the stories for him. He has chosen you. In your new pouch you must not place your hunting tools—you must place a stone inside it for every tale he tells."

So, all winter long, the young couple lived atop the cliff and listened to the wonderful tales. When spring came, Gaqka's pouch was full of stories, and he knew all the history of the olden days.

"Now that it is spring," said Gaqka's young wife, "we must go back to your own people. There, you will become a great man."

Gaqka's face lengthened. "We cannot go back," he said. "In my own country I am an outcast. They call me names and laugh at me."

The young wife gently took his hand. "You will see," she said confidently. "We must go north."

Taking the pouch of story-stones, Gaqka and his wife went down the cliff. Getting down was much easier than going up, Gaqka noticed. At the bottom, he saw that the canoe was still there.

The young wife smiled. "My canoe!" she exclaimed. Gaqka looked at her.

"Your canoe?" he asked.

"Yes," she said. "I sent it through the air to find you."

They pulled the canoe into the river. She climbed into the front, and Gaqka climbed into the back. He took the paddle, and plunged it into the water. The canoe moved slowly through the river at first— they were paddling against the current. But soon the canoe arose, and began gliding through the air.

When they reached the forest near Gaqka's village, the canoe came down.

"Now," said the young woman, "I will give you new clothes, clean you, and remove your hunting scars." She found a large, hollow log, and told Gaqka to crawl through it.

"How will this clean me?" he asked. "It will only make me even dirtier."

"Please try," she said. So he did. He came out the other side of the log dressed in fine clothing. He was a very handsome young man.

Arm in arm they walked to the village, and people came out to greet him. They did not recognize him as the orphan who left their village months ago. They took the couple in, and treated them with great generosity.

Finally, the young man told them who he was.

"I am the boy you once called 'Filth-Covered-One,'" he told them. "But I am different now. I forgive you for your misunderstanding. I have returned a great hunter and storyteller."

The people understood what he meant by "great hunter"—they saw the fine skins he wore. But "storyteller" meant nothing to them. Like everyone else who had never been to the top of the cliff, they had never heard stories before.

That night, the villagers gathered around Gaqka and his wife, and heard the tales he told. With each tale, Gaqka took a new stone out of the pouch, and with it came the story.

From then on, Gaqka told the tales the rock had told. He received many gifts from the villagers. The people honored Gaqka as a great man, and listened well to his stories.

Gaqka was the first human ever to tell tales of the ancient days. And people remembered his stories, told others, and have passed them on ever since.

Even this one.

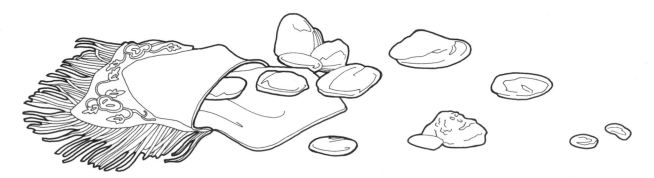

THE GHOST HUNTER

A Dakota Sioux Story

It was against the custom of the Dakota people to hunt alone. Dakota hunters usually traveled in groups, and when they captured large game they would all carry it back to the village and share it.

But one man's family was starving, and he could not take the chance of having to share anything he caught with anyone else. He decided to hunt alone, even though it meant going against the way of his people. He had to feed his family.

After a long journey into the forest, the man set up his camp amid a group of tall trees. He tried to sleep, but he tossed and turned, and eventually he awoke to a strange wailing sound. In front of him, a ghost appeared.

The ghost moaned in the voices of the man's wife and children. She was completely white. She wore a white deerskin dress, white moccasins, and cobwebs of white hair floated on her head. The hunter stared in fear.

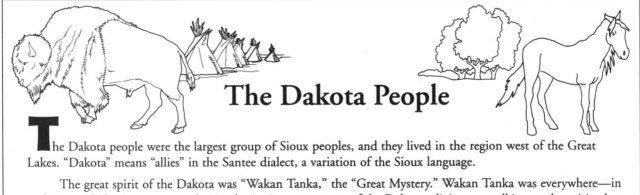

The Dakota People

The Dakota people were the largest group of Sioux peoples, and they lived in the region west of the Great Lakes. "Dakota" means "allies" in the Santee dialect, a variation of the Sioux language.

The great spirit of the Dakota was "Wakan Tanka," the "Great Mystery." Wakan Tanka was everywhere—in rocks, trees, lightning, songs, and animals. An important part of the Dakota religion was talking to the spirits, but not trying to control their responses, or to become one of them.

It was the Dakota people who defeated General Custer at Little Bighorn.

...ial feast

...lling, speech-

...dancing is an important tradition

...e American peoples of the Northwest

...thering like this one, called a potlatch, was often

...lebrate a marriage or birth. The host of a potlatch

...food, blankets, and other valuable gifts to his guests.

Then another ghost appeared. This ghost was dressed for mourning, in the way the Dakotas dressed for one who has died in dishonor. The man was petrified.

He said nothing, for he knew that ghosts could only speak if they were spoken to. The hunter got up and ran off as fast as he could, leaving behind his bow and arrows, and disappearing into the darkness.

He ran headfirst into another ghost.

This ghost looked like an old woman at first—and, on a closer look, like his own mother. She too was dressed in white, and she floated high in the air, crying white tears that fell upon him like snowflakes. The hunter dropped to his knees. The ghost of his mother floated above him, weeping.

Suddenly, a howl echoed through the forest. The ghost disappeared instantly, like a piece of pottery being smashed. The howl came again. Whatever it was, it was coming closer. The hunter shut his eyes in fear.

When he opened them, a man was pacing around the hunter. This man was speaking to him, but he could not understand what he was saying. It was a language he had never heard. The hunter watched the man's feet in confusion as he circled. They moved around in a circle many times, and very quickly.

The man who was pacing was becoming angry. The hunter still couldn't understand what he was saying, but his voice was cruel and low—almost growling. The hunter shut his eyes again.

He opened them again, and where before he had seen a man's moccasins circling, he now saw huge paws. The hunter looked up. A wolf was encircling him, growling deeply.

The wolf came forward to sniff the hunter. He smelled his moccasins. He sniffed his face. The man was frozen, and the wolf sensed his fear. But the hunter did not move.

About them, the night was still. The moon shone down directly on the man and the wolf. The hunter realized why the wolf was circling him, and why the ghosts had appeared—it was because he had broken the custom of his people and hunted alone.

Then the wolf bared its teeth. Growling loudly, the wolf grabbed the hunter's belt with his fangs. But he did not try to kill the hunter. He tugged at the belt, as if he wanted the hunter to follow. The hunter stood, and the wolf barked and walked just ahead of him. The wolf led him to a nearby camp.

There he found hunters from another tribe talking around a fire. They had lost one of their own hunters, and needed one more man to have a good hunt. The wolf stopped, looked at the lone hunter, looked at the group of hunters, and walked into the fire. He came out the other side unharmed—but he had turned into a man.

The man who had been a wolf went to talk to the group of hunters. The lone man could not hear what they were saying, but he saw everyone nodding and smiling. Then they called for the lone hunter to enter the fire circle and meet the others. As they talked, the man who had appeared from the fire backed into the forest darkness.

The next thing they all heard was a great howl—the strange man had become a wolf again and disappeared into the night.

The lone man joined the group of hunters, and never hunted alone again. He was treated well, and became the best hunter in the group. There was plenty of food for his family, and they lived comfortably.

From then on, every night after the hunt he left meat outside the camp, at the edge of the forest. And every morning the meat was gone—only the prints of a wolf remained.

THE RACE OF TURTLE AND BEAVER

A Seneca Story

A turtle once lived in a deep hole in the middle of a stream. He liked his home very much. The stream was small and quiet, and when he was cold he could cover himself with a mud blanket. There were many fish around for him to eat, and on the shore was a swamp he could visit.

One day, while he was out of his hole, exploring the swamp, it became very cold. It was getting late, and the turtle was tired. He swam back to his hole, and found a soft spot in the mud to bury himself.

"Here I will rest," he said to himself. And there he rested.

When he woke up and opened his eyes, something seemed different. The stream was completely still. He poked his head above water to see what had happened.

The turtle saw that the swamp had vanished! He climbed out of his mud bed and looked around for something familiar—but everything around looked different.

"Some magician has changed my home!" he exclaimed. Indeed, his little stream had become a great lake, and in the middle of the great lake was an island. The island was covered with sticks, and the turtle swam to it to get a closer look.

When the turtle crawled upon the island it made a hollow, creaking sound which frightened him and made him quickly slip back into the water. Confused and frightened, the turtle hid.

Soon, a dark shadow appeared in the water and rose to the surface. As the creature came up, Turtle poked his head from his hiding place and called out.

"Who are you?" he demanded, and quickly went back into hiding. Turtle heard a slap on the water, and then an answer.

"I am Beaver," said the creature, "Who are you?"

Turtle did not respond right away. He understood now. The beaver had cut up all the branches in the swamp, and blocked up the stream, making this great lake.

Then Turtle heard a voice from behind him say, "Get out of my way!"

Turtle turned around and saw Beaver dragging a branch. He swam aside to let the beaver pass, and the branch nearly hit him in the head.

"You would think," said Turtle, "that I should be the one who says, 'Get out of my way.'"

Beaver dove under the island with the branch and then came back up. "Who made *you* owner of the stream?" he asked.

"This is my home," said Turtle angrily. "I have lived here for a long time."

Beaver laughed, and his big teeth clicked together.

"Ha! If this is your home," he said, waving his tail around, "where is your house? I see my house, but not yours."

Turtle did not answer. "How did you get here?" he asked.

"I came here to build this dam," Beaver replied, "and I made this lake. Now I have built a home here too."

Turtle was very angry, but he stayed calm. "I came here long

ago," said the turtle, "and built a fishing hole in this stream. You have no right to ruin my home."

Beaver slapped his tail against the water impatiently.

"I am going to break down your dam and restore my home," Turtle told Beaver, and started underwater.

Beaver stopped him. "That would do no good," he said. "I will build another dam. Then I will call my brothers, and we will guard this place and keep you away."

Turtle thought for a moment. "How can we settle this?" he asked.

Beaver thought too, chewing on a stick. "We will see who can stay underwater the longest," he said.

"That would be too easy for me," Turtle said, fairly. "I could sleep for a year underwater."

"Then," said Beaver, "I propose that we run a race."

Turtle agreed. "Whoever wins will stay here, and the loser will

The Seneca People

The word "Seneca" means "People of the Big Hill." This could refer to a large hill in New York State just south of Canandaigua Lake. The Seneca people lived in the Northeast and Midwest, around Lake Erie, and today they live throughout the Northeast.

The Seneca people were members of the League of Five Nations—an independent group of five Indian peoples who agreed to work together in matters of defense. The Seneca decided who could join the League and who could not, and so they were known as the "doorkeepers"—or "Honennihohonte."

go. We will start at the far shore, and swim across to the other bank."

They both swam to shore and prepared to begin—but Turtle had a plan.

"We will start," said Turtle, "when I bite down on your tail. Then I will let go, and we will race." Beaver agreed, even though there was a strange, wicked gleam in Turtle's eyes.

Turtle bit down on Beaver's tail, and Beaver started across. But the clever turtle hung onto Beaver's tail, and was dragged along with him.

As they neared the shore, Beaver looked around for Turtle. Finally, he saw Turtle behind him, clinging to his tail.

"So there you are!" he said. "But it doesn't matter. You are still behind me, and I will win the race." He was almost at the far bank.

Just then, Turtle bit down hard, and Beaver barked in pain, swishing his tail to shake the turtle off.

But Turtle bit down even harder. Beaver did not like this at all, so with all his strength he flopped his tail over his head. Turtle went with it.

Then, Turtle let go. He flew through the air past the beaver, over the stream, and landed squarely on the shore—ahead of Beaver.

Turtle stood confidently on the shore, and looked out over the lake.

"I have won this race," he called to Beaver. "You must go away. This is once again my home."

Beaver tried to think of something to say, but he could not. He had lost. He swam back to the island to nurse his sore tail, and to take apart the dam.

Turtle had outwitted him.

THE SUN TRAP

A Tête de Boule Story

Long ago lived a boy named Tcikabis who liked to climb trees. He could climb better than anyone else. But Tcikabis also had a special power—he could climb to the top of a tall tree, and then, by blowing on it with all his might, he could make the tree grow higher. He could then climb to the new top, and repeat the process. This way, Tcikabis could climb higher than anyone.

One day, he climbed higher than he had ever gone before. He climbed so high that he saw a straight, wide path across the top of the sky.

Who can it be that travels upon such a wide path? he thought to himself. *I must find out. I will stretch myself across the path and go to sleep. When someone comes by, I will awaken and see him.* The high climb had tired him out, and he quickly fell asleep.

Soon he was awakened by footsteps on the road. *Now I will find out who travels here*, Tcikabis thought. He looked up, and saw only a bright light. He covered his eyes, and realized that the sun itself was approaching!

"Out of my way," ordered the sun.

"Go around me," Tcikabis yawned, not moving.

"I cannot leave my path!" the sun said, becoming hot with anger. "If you do not get out of my way, I will burn you!"

But Tcikabis was not frightened. He laughed, and said, "Jump over me."

The sun stepped over him, but as he did, Tcikabis nearly died of the heat. His clothes were all burned, and he was badly scorched. Tcikabis was angry, and he returned to the earth to plan his revenge.

Back on the ground, Tcikabis plotted. He made a large net, and his sister asked him what it was for.

"I am going to get even with the sun," Tcikabis said. He was so angry he could not think clearly. He did not remember that he had blocked the sun's path. His sister tried to warn him against the trick, but he would not listen.

With his net on his back, Tcikabis climbed back up the tree to the path, and set the trap. Soon, the sun approached on his daily journey, and became caught in the net. Darkness covered the world.

Tcikabis was happy that his trap had worked, and the darkness continued for some time.

But people were becoming angry. Without light, they couldn't get anything done. Plants could not grow. And no one could see the world's beauty.

Tcikabis realized that it would always be dark unless he freed the sun. But how could he free the sun without burning himself? He knew too well how much damage the sun could do.

Then he had an idea—he could ask an animal to cut through the net! The sun's heat might not reach tiny creatures. He called together all the small animals—mice, rabbits, frogs, turtles, squirrels, and others—and they climbed the great tree.

One by one, the animals tried to bite through the net. Turtle crawled up, and extended his neck to bite through the trap. As he stretched out his neck, the heat of the sun became too great, and burned him. Rabbit tried next. He hopped up cautiously, but the heat was too strong for him, too, and his whiskers were scorched. One by one, the animals tried and failed.

Finally it was the mouse's turn. He crept up underneath the net—and began to chew through. He was so small that the sun's heat did not reach him. At length, the mouse freed the sun.

The sun came out slowly, stretched, and continued along the path as if nothing had ever happened.

And the world was light again.

HOW BUTTERFLIES CAME TO BE

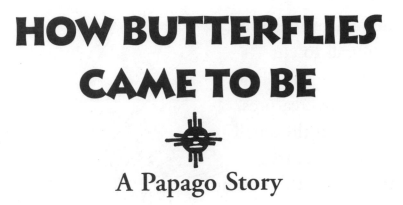

A Papago Story

One spring day, not long after the world was made, the Creator sat and watched the world. He smiled as the children and animals played together. It was a good world, and its creatures were happy. But then he had a sad thought.

He realized that some day, the children who were playing so joyfully would grow old. He thought about how all things get older and die, and about how winter would come. The Creator became very gloomy.

Then he heard the children laughing, and saw the sun shining down on them warmly. He realized that today it was still spring, and that life was good. He decided to do something to preserve the beautiful colors that surrounded the world—something to help him keep the warm feeling that he had.

In a bag, the Creator gathered spots of color from everything around bright yellow from the sun and a gorgeous blue from the sky, a vivid green from the tree leaves, and a palette of colors from the flowers. Then, to complete the mixture, he gathered the songs of birds.

56

The Creator shook the bag to mix the contents, and presented it to the gleeful children.

When they opened it, hundreds and hundreds of colored butterflies flew out, singing a beautiful song. They looked like color in motion, fluttering around on the gentle breezes. They sang even more beautifully than the birds. The Creator smiled wide, and the children stared in awe.

Overhead, a songbird flew by to see what was happening. She saw the joyful scene below, but did not feel happy. She was angry with the Creator for giving away her song. She swooped down.

"Creator," said the bird, flapping her wings impatiently, "You have made wonderful things, and I thank you. But it isn't right to give away our songs to butterflies. Their beauty is their color, and that is enough."

The Creator thought. *The butterflies sing melodically,* he thought, *but they do seem to overshadow the other creatures.*

The Papago People

More than a hundred years ago, the Papago Indians of the Southwest United States lived at the bases of canyons, along the rivers that ran through the canyons.

The canyon walls were good protection—they kept out strangers. But the Papago often felt isolated from other tribes. They had a belief in the importance of journeys, and they welcomed outsiders for their news and their ideas.

He decided that all creatures should have equal beauty.

"You are right," said the Creator. And with that, he took the songs from the butterflies. They have been silent ever since.

"The music of the butterflies has stopped," said the Creator, "but they are beautiful just the same." And indeed they are.

THE TRICKSTER WHO WANTED TO FLY

An Assiniboine Story

One autumn day, the trickster Iktome looked up into the white sky. He saw some geese flying by in a V shape.

Now, Iktome was a very powerful trickster. But he could not do everything, even though he thought he could. He was not much of a hunter, for example. He always had to fool the animals into giving him food. In fact, he wasn't really that good at anything—except trickery. Everything he received, everything he could do, was because of his cunning.

Usually, Iktome could survive quite well with the unwitting help of others. But this life had a bad side, too. Iktome had gained a reputation as a trickster— so no one trusted him.

Iktome was not thinking about this right now. He was thinking that he wanted to fly.

"I'd like to fly with you!"

The Trickster

Tricksters are the con artists of Native American folklore, and every Indian culture has tales of its trickster. Coyote, Raven, Crow, and Hare are only a few of the forms the trickster takes. One famous trickster is Iktome (or Unktomee).

In many legends, tricksters are combinations of god and animal. They often have magical powers, but like humans, they also have problems. They are greedy. They are vain. They are selfish.

Tricksters show all of us why the world is imperfect. They show us how we act foolishly— and help us correct our faults.

It's the trickster's role to keep us on our toes.

he called to the geese as they passed directly overhead.

"That would be lovely," said the head goose, suspiciously. "But flying is difficult. Especially difficult without wings, and you have none."

Iktome was frustrated. "I don't care," he said. "I want to fly!" He sounded like an angry child.

The lead goose spoke with the other geese. They didn't believe Iktome was telling the truth. He had tricked them many times before.

"What should we do?" asked the lead goose.

"This is a good chance for us to get back at Iktome for all of his tricks," one of the other geese said. "I have a plan." He whispered it to the lead goose, as Iktome watched from below.

They all came to an agreement, and swooped down toward Iktome. Eight of the geese landed on Iktome, grabbing him by his head, his shoulders, his arms, and his legs. With some trouble, and a lot of flapping, they lifted him into the sky.

Iktome was overjoyed. He was actually flying! "This is great!" he told them. The world looked so small from up there. The rivers looked like tiny creeks. The trees looked like bushes. The bears looked like chipmunks, and the chipmunks looked like ants.

"Higher!" Iktome cried. "Higher!" So the geese took him higher. But Iktome was never satisfied. He always wanted more.

"Let me fly by myself, now that I know how it is done," he said to the geese.

Though he wanted to trick Iktome, the lead goose did not want Iktome to hurt himself. "You have no wings, my friend," he told Iktome. "You will fall."

"I see how you do it. It is so simple. Let me try," Iktome insisted.

So, the geese let go.

Iktome flapped as hard as he could. He kicked his legs. He stretched out his body so that he would glide on the wind. And he flew—at least, that was what Iktome expected to happen.

What actually happened was this: as soon as the geese let go, Iktome fell fast toward the ground. The geese chased him through the air, and grabbed him just before he hit a large rock. They took him back up into the sky.

"That was close," said Iktome. "What was I doing wrong?"

The lead goose explained. "You are not doing anything wrong. You are not a goose. You are Iktome. You cannot fly."

But Iktome would not listen. "I must fly. Because I am Iktome, I must fly. I can do everything better than everyone else."

The geese were sick of Iktome's bragging. Besides, they were tired of carrying him all over the sky. So they gave him his wish. They let him go again.

Again Iktome flapped and flapped. He kicked his legs. He glided through the air—straight down into a mud hole.

Iktome was back on the ground. And he was stuck.

Above him, the geese laughed. "Well," the lead goose said, "I don't know if you can do *everything* better than everyone else, but you certainly can get stuck better." With that, the geese flew off into the sun.

The trickster had been tricked.

When Iktome finally got out of the hole, after several days of struggling, he was very tired. But this was not going to be a good day for him.

Iktome rested on a rock to catch his breath. As he sat down, the rock moved. Iktome could not get comfortable on it.

"Pardon me, rock, but I would like to rest for a moment. Would you mind not moving around so much?" Iktome said.

The rock spoke back. "How would you like it if I sat on you?"

"But I am tired," said Iktome. "Please let me relax."

The rock did not answer right away. It looked as if it was thinking. (Rocks always look as if they're thinking.)

"You may rest," the rock finally answered. "But you must give me a gift."

"Agreed," said Iktome, knowing that he had nothing to give. And he rested. Finally, Iktome wanted to get up. But he could not. He was stuck to the rock!

"Where is my gift?" asked the rock, as Iktome tried in vain to stand.

"I do not have it with me," Iktome said. "It is back at my lodge. If you release me, I will return with it."

But the rock knew that Iktome was not to be trusted. "If I release you," the rock said, "you will be long gone. I will hold you until you give me the gift."

For four long days, Iktome stayed stuck to the rock, trying ever so often to free himself. But he could not.

Then, the geese who had helped him fly passed overhead. "My friends, please help me get free," he called to them.

But again, the geese were suspicious of him. They thought he only wanted to get back at them for leaving him in a mud hole.

"We cannot help," they honked back.

"If you do help me, I will give you any daughter I have."

The geese thought about this, and agreed that it was a fair bargain. Down they flew toward the ground, passing right over Iktome and the rock, causing a strong wind to move them. The rock shook a bit.

Up they went again. And down they came again, faster, making more wind than before. The rock moved more. Over and over again they repeated this, until finally the wind was so strong that Iktome blew right off the rock.

As the geese landed to claim their gift, Iktome thanked them.

But then he started to walk away.

"Wait!" they called. "What about our gift?"

"I told you that I would give you any daughter that I have," Iktome said, smugly. "But I have no daughter."

The geese were speechless. Laughing, Iktome ran off into the hills.

WHY WE SLEEP

A Chippewa Story

Sleep is mysterious. No one knows why we have to sleep, or what makes us feel tired. But the Chippewa people have an explanation.

They say that there is a spirit called Weeng, who commands hundreds and hundreds of tiny, invisible creatures. These tiny people are everywhere, especially around trees and lodges, and they are always awake and ready for action.

Each of these beings is armed with a club. When one of these creatures sees a person relaxing, or lying down, he carefully climbs up on his forehead, and hits the person with the club.

The blow does not hurt, but it does make a person feel sleepy. A second blow makes a person move slowly, and sometimes causes him to close his eyes. A third blow causes a deep sleep.

This is the job of these creatures—to put everyone they meet to sleep. They sometimes hide in hunters' pouches, and when the hunter sits to smoke a pipe, or to eat, the creatures come out and put him to sleep. This helps to protect animals from the hunter.

Mostly, these creatures are friendly. They put people to sleep to give them more energy when they awaken. But sometimes, like all creatures, they make mistakes or play pranks, and sometimes these pranks are

dangerous. For example, these creatures have been known to hit people as they float in canoes.

Weeng himself is less understood. But once, a great hunter named Iagoo is said to have come close to meeting Weeng.

One day, Iagoo went out with his dogs to hunt. Along the way, he passed through a thick brush, and when he came out, his dogs were nowhere to be found.

Iagoo was alarmed and confused—his dogs were faithful animals, and he was very attached to them. He called to them at the top of his lungs, and searched the thicket for hours.

Finally, he came to a spot deep within the brush, and saw the dogs sleeping soundly. He tried to arouse his dogs.

But Iagoo himself was getting sleepy. He decided to lie down for a quick nap. It is said that as Iagoo was drifting off to sleep he saw a spirit perched in the branches of a tree above him. This spirit was shaped like a giant butterfly, and made a low, soothing murmur, like the sound of a distant stream. Then the creature disappeared, and all went dark.

It is not known if this was truly where Weeng dwelled—Iagoo was known to make up stories from time to time, as all great warriors do.

This is all we know of sleep.

STEALING SUMMER

An Assiniboine Story

Long ago, the whole earth was covered with snow. The trickster Iktome was called to the sky by some supernatural beings to help them get rid of the snow.

"If you help us," they told him, "We will give you powers to fool people, and to make anything you want talk—except the water."

Iktome liked nothing better than to fool people, and he liked the idea of being able to make things talk. *Someday that might be a useful thing*, he thought.

"I will help," he promised.

"That is good," said one of the beings. "Far in the east, beyond the reaches of the snow, is a man who keeps the summer. You are to steal the good weather from his lodge. It is tied to a pole there."

"Simple," said Iktome, and started off.

"Just a moment," said the being. "The owner of the lodge is very clever. He has senses you do not possess. He can tell without even looking whenever anyone comes to the lodge. Birds are his servants, and they keep guard."

Iktome did not look quite so confident now.

"He has promised that he would not try to take the summer back if someone steals it from him. But until that day, summer will stay with him, and it will be winter where you dwell," the being explained.

Iktome thought hard. "If I try to help you," he said, "then I must have the power to make things talk right away."

The beings agreed. "I will get summer back," Iktome said. And with that, he went down to the earth.

Iktome first went to the highest spot in the snow-covered land. It was cold, and the air was thin, so he built a fire. Soon, a jackrabbit passed by, feeling the warmth.

"Brother," Iktome said, "come here." The rabbit hopped over. "Have you seen any other animals around here?"

"Yes," said the rabbit, rubbing his paws in the heat, "I have seen Wolf, Coyote, Red Fox, and some birds."

"Good," said Iktome. "Tell them to come see me, for I am their brother."

The rabbit nodded, stood for a moment to warm himself again, and ran off to deliver the message.

The next morning, all the animals came to see Iktome on the tip of the mountain. "My brothers and sisters," he said to them. "I ask for your help. I am on a quest for summer. We must find the keeper of the summer weather, steal it, and bring it to the snow-covered land."

The animals were confused. Because they had lived in the snow country all their lives, they didn't know what Iktome meant.

"What is summer?" asked one of the birds.

"Just do as I say," replied Iktome, "and it will be good for all of us. We begin tonight."

For some reason, this satisfied the animals.

That night, they set off toward the east. The snow seemed to stretch on forever. They traveled for many months. Finally, when it seemed as if all was lost, they reached the end of the snow. The snow just stopped, like a great sea of white coming to meet the land. There, Iktome planted a long pole, and set a fast-flying bird on top of the pole. The animals sat around the pole.

"Can you see the lodge?" Iktome asked the bird.

"Yes," the bird replied. "It is far off. But not further than we have already gone."

"Good," replied Iktome. Then he spoke to the owl. "You will fly ahead to the front of the lodge, and we will come from behind. But be very careful. Fly to the smoke hole and look in to see where the good weather is tied up, but don't let the owner see you!" The owl flew off.

Iktome addressed the other animals. "We will soon have the summer back, my brothers and sisters. You have traveled well." And so Wolf, Coyote, Red Fox, and Iktome set off.

The owl reached the tipi safely, and alighted on the pole that came up from its center. He looked in, and there was the owner, staring straight up at him.

"What are you doing?" the man asked angrily. The owl did not reply. He was nervous, and looked frantically for the good weather.

The man took a long stick from the fire, and struck the owl's beak, burning him. The owl flew off in pain. "I wonder what that bird was trying to do," the owner said. Then he called one of his servants to keep watch outside.

Iktome waited at the edge of the summer land. When the owl

returned, they soothed his burnt beak.

"The good weather is in a bag inside the lodge," said the owl. "But the owner always keeps it by his side. Outside, one of his servants keeps guard."

"You have done well," said Iktome. "Now it is my turn. Red Fox, you will help me. I'll wear a fox skin to disguise myself and distract the servant. Then you can jump in and steal the bag of good weather."

Iktome and the fox walked toward the lodge. The servant saw them coming, but he was not surprised to see two foxes. As they neared the servant, a wind came up, and blew the skin off Iktome. The servant recognized him immediately.

"Iktome is coming!" he began to shout. But he never finished. Iktome threw a sticky paste in his mouth, and closed it tight. Then they tied him up.

"Now," Iktome whispered to the fox, "you crawl in from the rear, snatch the bag, and run out. The owner will chase you, but run through my legs to the other animals. I have a plan to delay him. As

Native American Homes

In this story, the owner of "the good weather" lives in a lodge, but Native Americans made their homes in a variety of dwellings.

Nomadic, wandering peoples often lived in tipis (teepees). This word comes from the Sioux word meaning "to dwell." Most tipis were cone-shaped tents with covers of buffalo hide.

soon as you reach the edge of the summer country, pass the bag to the next animal in line, and have each one do the same."

Iktome waited at some distance while the fox crawled into the lodge. The owner was asleep, facing the front, and his senses did not warn him of his visitor.

The Fox saw the bag, and grabbed it. It was heavy, and made a loud sound as the fox dragged it off. The owner woke.

"Stop!" he cried, and began to chase his uninvited guest.

The fox ran fast, and passed between Iktome's legs. Just as he did, Iktome reached underneath and through his legs, coming up with the fox skin in his hands.

"No need to run any more, brother," he said to the owner of the lodge. "I have caught him!" He held up the skin.

The owner was confused. He took the skin in his hands. "You must have sat on him," he said.

Other wandering peoples, such as the Algonquins, lived in tent-like houses called wigwams. These were more substantial than tipis. The word wigwam comes from the word "wekuwomut," meaning "in his house."

In the Southwest, Pueblo peoples lived in cliff dwellings, apartment-style brick complexes that were built right into caves along the sides of cliffs.

Iktome pretended to be confused as well. "Hmmm. He must have left his skin behind and gone somewhere underground. I will help you look for him."

Of course, they did not find him underground. Or behind the lodge. Or in the bushes. The fox was nowhere to be found—and the bag was gone too!

"This is very strange," said Iktome. "I was certain I had him. We had better sit for a while and think about it."

The owner agreed, because Iktome had the power to trick anyone. For a few minutes, they sat and discussed the matter. They even took time to smoke a pipe.

But after a while, out of the side of his eye, the owner saw the fox reach the other animals. He saw Fox give the bag to Wolf, who ran on and passed it to Coyote. Coyote ran swiftly and passed the bag to Jackrabbit. Jackrabbit held the bag in his mouth and took it to the edge of the snow.

The man who had been keeping the summer weather jumped up. "I see the fox!" he cried, running as fast as he could toward the animals. Iktome sat and watched, laughing to himself. Just as the owner reached the other animals, they all disappeared into holes underground. The owner did not know what to do.

Then he saw Jackrabbit clutching the bag near the end of the snowbank. He ran toward him—but he was too late. The fast-flying bird swooped down from his pole and carried the bag off into the sky.

Quickly, the owner called to his guard birds.

"Stop that bird!" he yelled to them. But the bird had crossed over into the land of the snow, and was flying close to the ground so that the birds could not find him. After some time, the birds returned to the owner of the lodge and admitted that they had failed. The owner jumped up and down in a rage, and decided to return to his lodge.

Iktome saw the owner coming back, and he sprinkled water on his face to look as if he had been sweating.

"Did you. . ." he paused, pretending he had to catch his breath, ". . . Did you catch him? I tried to find him—I practically wore myself out! I'm so angry!" And he took his knife and plunged it into the ground in false anger.

"I will kill the thief when I find him!" Iktome swore. "Let's go track him."

But the owner of the lodge was too tired. "No, I need rest. Maybe the fox put the bag back. You go chase them." He went inside to sleep. He had been beaten.

Iktome laughed to himself when the owner turned his back. "I promise I will find them!" he said, unable to keep from smiling. Then he turned, and ran off to the nearby mountains.

There, on the summit of the highest mountain, the animals waited, seated around a fire.

"Good work, brethren!" he said. "We have it now. Bring the bag down," he called to the fast-flying bird who was circling above. The bird glided down and set the bag at Iktome's feet.

"Now, let us hope this is the right one," he said, untying the knot."

As he spread the bag open, the snow upon which they were seated began to disappear. It didn't melt—it just seemed to fade, as the light does as the sun goes down. They looked about them. The trees, which had been no more than white statues, had turned green, and started to sprout leaves. Iktome and the animals smiled.

"I think this is indeed the right one," he said. "We deserve a reward. Let us eat a warrior's feast." And, gathering the food that now was plentiful around them, they did. Then they all slept, preparing for their long journey home.

When morning came and they were all ready to leave, Iktome tied up the bag to travel more easily. As he closed it, the snow returned.

"Let us go home," he said. Down the mountain they went, slipping in the snow and shivering in the cold. Since they now knew what it meant to be warm, winter seemed more harsh than it had been before. The animals began to complain.

"Quiet, my brothers," Iktome said. "I will see what I can do. Pointing the bag directly ahead of them, Iktome opened it just a little. Ahead of the group, a path of bare ground cleared for them in the middle of the snow. Tiny flowers poked up.

"Is this better?" he asked. The animals nodded. They all walked on.

Soon, Wolf and Fox began to complain. "Our feet are sore," they told Iktome. "The bare ground is hard on them."

Iktome sighed, becoming annoyed, and closed the bag. The snow returned.

All the way home, Iktome opened and closed the bag depending upon whose feet were sore, who was too cold, and who complained loudest. By the time they reached their homes, Iktome was exhausted by the constant complaining.

"We must call a council of all the animals," he said, "to decide whether it should be winter or summer."

So he called together all the creatures, and asked them what kind of weather they wanted.

The frog wanted it to be summer always. The beaver wanted winter for three months, and summer for nine months. The rabbit wanted winter for nine months, and summer for three. Every animal wanted something different.

Finally, the wise turtle spoke up. He smoked his pipe, and puffed as the words came out.

"There should be six months of summer, and six months of winter. But halfway through each season, you should open or close the bag a bit each day, so that the change is slow. That way, it won't be too cold or too warm."

The animals all agreed that this was a good solution. And even though he hadn't thought of it, Iktome also liked the turtle's idea.

It's good that I made them able to speak, he thought, *or we'd never know what to do.* That was Iktome—never doing any of the work, but always taking the credit. That was Iktome, the trickster.

HUMMINGBIRD AND CRANE

A Cherokee Story

Hummingbird and Crane were always arguing.

If it wasn't one thing, it was another, but it usually came down to this: Crane thought that she owned the river, and Hummingbird thought that she did.

They agreed to settle matters once and for all in a great race.

"We will race for four days," said Crane, sounding superior, "and on the fourth day, whoever reaches the dead tree at the bank of the river first will own all the water in the river."

Hummingbird buzzed in agreement. She knew that she was faster than Crane, even though she was smaller. But she didn't realize that Crane had more energy, and could fly for days without resting.

The time came for the race, and off they flew. Crane immediately took off into the air at full speed. Hummingbird took her time, flitting from flower to flower, tasting each blossom as she pleased. She knew that she could overtake Crane at any time.

When Crane was way ahead, Hummingbird decided to pass her. She buzzed by, almost clipping Crane in the head. Hummingbird flew out of sight.

I will never win this way, thought Crane.

But Crane didn't have to worry for long. Hummingbird had found a colorful field of wildflowers, and was tasting every one. Crane flew past again. Not long after, however, Hummingbird overtook Crane once more.

Night was coming, so Hummingbird rested and slept in a patch of bluebells. But Crane travelled all night. She was long past Hummingbird's resting spot when Hummingbird woke the next day.

Hummingbird was so swift that she caught up with Crane by the time the sun had reached the sky's midpoint. She kept her lead—until she found more flowers. Then Crane passed her. After a time, Hummingbird passed Crane again. The race went on like this until the eve of the fourth day, when Hummingbird rested again.

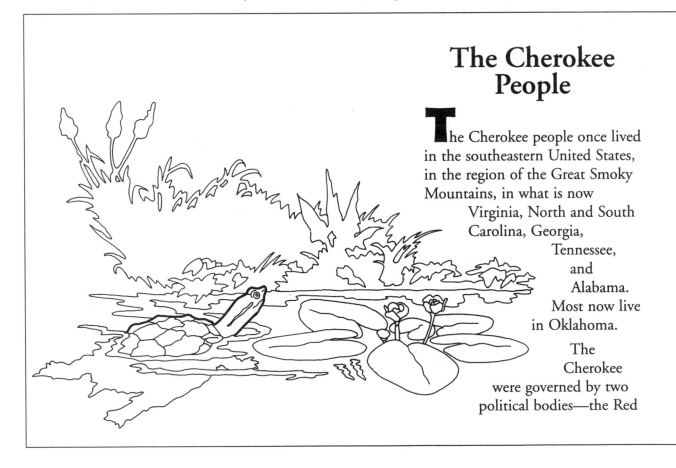

The Cherokee People

The Cherokee people once lived in the southeastern United States, in the region of the Great Smoky Mountains, in what is now Virginia, North and South Carolina, Georgia, Tennessee, and Alabama. Most now live in Oklahoma.

The Cherokee were governed by two political bodies—the Red

I have no need to worry, she thought to herself. *Even though it is almost the fourth day, I will beat Crane in the morning.* So she slept soundly.

The next morning, when Hummingbird woke, she fluttered casually toward the dead tree across the river. After stopping once more, Hummingbird reached the tree—and found Crane sitting below it.

"All of the water is now mine," said Crane. And she went to drink in her river. From then on, Hummingbird drank only from the flowers she passed.

And it is still that way today.

organization, which governed in times of war, and the White organization, which governed in times of peace.

The word "Cherokee" probably comes from the Choctaw word meaning "cave people."

THE TRICKSTER AND HIS BUNDLE OF SONGS

A Sioux Story

One bright day, a flock of ducks was flying north. The journey was long and tiring, so they stopped to rest beside a small lake.

The ducks were having a good time playing and splashing in the water. It was a good day to be alive.

Suddenly, one of the ducks stopped playing. She saw a strange-looking creature coming toward them, carrying a huge load. As the creature got closer, she saw that it was a little old man carrying a large bag.

Portrait of a Trickster

Names: Coyote; Old Man Coyote; Iktome; Unktomee

Profession: Trickster; also Creator

Personality: Well meaning; sometimes lazy. As the Trickster, gets others to do his work. Careless. Likes to amuse himself.

Known for: His howl and his laughter. His cry tells us that he understands that the world is a crazy place.

His Purpose: The Trickster shows us our darker sides—that we all have part of the trickster in us.

By now, all the ducks had stopped playing to see what was going on. The old man sat down. He was the trickster, Unktomee, in disguise! And he was hungry.

"What have you got there?" asked the duck who first saw Unktomee.

"Got where?" said the old man. Unktomee was up to his old tricks. He needed food, and the ducks were just what he wanted.

"That bundle, there," said another duck. They all waddled out of the water to see.

"Oh, this!" said Unktomee. "It is only a bundle of songs. Nothing important." He stretched out on the ground to rest.

But the ducks were curious—just what Unktomee wanted. They flapped about and quacked, pleading, "Sing us one of your songs from the bundle!"

Unktomee sat up, smiling strangely. Then he began to build a small tipi with sticks from the land around them. For a roof, he took dry grass from the bundle, and attached it to the top of the tipi.

"There, it is done," he said. "Now come inside, and I will sing you a song."

The ducks crowded into the tipi. It was a tight fit, but they all made it. Unktomee stood by the door, outside.

He began to sing:

Ishtogmus wachee po!

Tuwa etowan kin

Ishtah ne sha kta!

which meant, "Dance with your eyes closed! Whoever opens them will have red eyes forever!"

The foolish ducks listened carefully to the song, keeping their eyes closed. One by one as he sang, he grabbed the ducks and shoved them into the empty bag. They were so busy dancing and listening that they didn't even have a chance to quack for help.

The ducks still inside the tipi did not notice that their friends were missing. They just kept their eyes closed, and enjoyed the music.

Finally, when just a few ducks were left, the duck who had first seen the old man felt that something was very wrong. She cracked her eyes open, and saw Unktomee, now out of his disguise, grab one of the other ducks and shove him into a large, moving bag.

She opened her eyes all the way in terror. "Fly! Fly!" she cried, "He will kill us all!"

The remaining ducks all opened their eyes wide, and rose up with a huge clamor of flapping wings and quacking. The tipi fell to the ground in pieces, and the few remaining ducks escaped.

"You have tricked us," they cried as they flew off. And that was not all—their eyes had turned red.

This is why some ducks have red eyes.

THE WARRIOR WHO WAS NEVER AFRAID

A Brule Sioux Story

One winter night, four ghosts sat talking, as ghosts so often do. They laughed their ghostly laughs, and smoked their ghost pipes, and talked about their favorite ghost topic—scaring people.

Each ghost thought himself the scariest one, and they took turns bragging about their frightful experiences—until one ghost brought up a topic that was scary even for them.

"They say," said the first ghost, "that there is a warrior who isn't afraid of anything—not even us."

"Not possible," said the second ghost. "I could frighten him."

"Me too," said the third ghost. "We should try."

"We should bet on it," said the fourth ghost. "That will make the challenge more exciting."

All the ghosts agreed that whoever scared the young man first would win the others' ghost horses. They found out where he walked at night, and waited until he came along.

The young man who was never afraid was whistling to himself as he came along his usual path. It was a beautiful, dark blue night, and the moon shone brightly. Suddenly, right in front of him, the first ghost appeared, taking the form of a skeleton.

"*Hellooooooo*," said the ghost, rattling his bones.

"Helloooooooo yourself," said the young man. "Out of my way. I want to get by."

"I will let you by," wailed the ghost, "but only after we have played a hoop and stick game. If you lose, you'll become a skeleton, too."

The young man laughed, "Whatever you say," and bent the skeleton into a loop. Then he borrowed a leg from the skeleton for a stick, and rolled the skeleton along, faster and faster.

"Oh! *OW!* Hey! St—STOP IT! *That hurt!*" moaned the skeleton as he bumped into rocks and trees.

"It looks like I won," said the young man.

"You hurt me," whimpered the ghost.

"You're the one who wanted to play," said the young man. With that, he kicked aside the ghost's skull and continued on his way, whistling.

Not far away he met the second ghost, who also took the form of a skeleton. The second ghost jumped right in front of him.

"*BOOOOOOOOO!*" the ghost shrieked.

"Same to you," said the young man, not impressed.

The ghost was disappointed, but he did not give up.

The Sioux People

The name Sioux comes from a word meaning "snake" or "enemy." The Sioux people are divided into three groups: Lakota, Dakota, and Nakota.

Many of the best-known Indians—Sitting Bull, Crazy Horse, and Red Cloud—were Lakota Sioux.

"Shall we dance?" the ghost asked.

"Delighted," said the young man. "Now, let's see—what should we use for a drum and stick?" He pretended to look around, and then stared at the ghost's bony skull. "I've got it!"

He grabbed the ghost's skull and a leg bone, and began beating the skull, singing a loud song and marching around.

"Cut it out!" shouted the drum. "I don't feel like dancing this way—and now I have a headache."

The young man rolled his eyes. "Ghosts can't feel pain," he said, putting the skull back on the skeleton.

"Well *I* do," said the ghost, rubbing his skull.

"What a whiner," said the young man. "Go whine elsewhere." He kicked the ghost in the chest, and sent his bones flying.

"Now look at me!" said the skull after it stopped rolling.

"Pull yourself together," said the young man, laughing at his own joke. "Goodbye!" And on he went.

Soon, as you might guess, he met the third ghost.

"This is getting old very quickly," muttered the young man. "Don't I know you?"

"We haven't met," said the third skeleton. "Those were my cousins." There was a pause. "Want to wrestle? If I win, you'll become a skeleton, too."

The young man thought. "Nah," he said. "I don't like wrestling. I feel like going sledding." He pointed to a nearby hill. "There's enough snow over there," he said, and he grabbed the ghost's rib cage.

When he got to the top of the hill, the young man sat down hard on the ghost's ribs. Then he shoved off. "This is great!" he said, plummeting down the hill.

"Gre—*Ow!*—Great for who?" asked the ghost. "You're breaking my ribs."

"You ghosts just can't take it," said the young man. "But you do look funny without any ribs. I think you should stay that way." He threw the ghost's ribs into a stream.

"Hey, those are mine!" yelled the ghost. "Now what do I do?"

"Dive," said the young man. "You look like you could use a bath, anyway. I'm sure the ghost women will like you better."

The ghost looked insulted, as much as a skeleton can. "I *am* a woman," she said.

"Huh!" said the young man. "You skeletons are all the same to me." And he walked on.

Soon, he heard a strange galloping noise: "Clip-clop-rattle-rattle, clip-clop-rattle-rattle." It was coming closer.

Out of the trees jumped the fourth skeleton ghost, riding a huge skeleton horse.

"I'm not scared," said the young man.

"*I'm not here to scare you,*" said the ghost. "*I'm here to kill you.*"

But the young man still was not afraid. "Then I'll scare you," he said. He gritted his teeth and made horrible faces. He rolled his eyes into the back of his head and shrieked a nasty shriek.

The skeleton was spooked, and tried to turn his horse around to gallop away. The young man grabbed the reins.

"Ah, a skeleton horse is exactly what I've been looking for," he said. "I'm tired of walking." With that, he yanked the skeleton off his skeleton saddle, dashed him into a thousand pieces, and rode off to his camp.

Indeed, it seemed that nothing could scare this young warrior!

It was very early in the morning when the young man rode into his camp. The sun had almost come up, but it was still dark. As he passed the river at the end of the camp, some women who were fetching water saw him riding the skeleton horse. They screamed in fright, and awakened the entire village.

The young man just laughed, and when the sun came up, the skeleton horse disappeared.

"I must be the bravest person ever," bragged the young warrior. No one disagreed, although they wished that they were still asleep.

Just then, the young man felt something creeping up his arm. He looked, and saw a tiny spider. The young man froze.

"G—g—get th—th—this thing off me! *I h—h—hate spiders!*" He couldn't move. He was shaking in fright.

The littlest girl in the village came up to him, looked at the spider, and plucked it off. The young man fainted.

With the spider in her palm, the little girl walked off to show her discovery to her friends.

THE SEASONS

A Chippewa Story

In a lodge by the edge of a frozen stream, an old man sat alone. Winter was ending, and his fire was nearly out.

The man looked as ancient as the mountains, and he was very pale. His hair was white with age, and his bones shook when he moved. He met each day with loneliness—he never had visitors, and the only sound he ever heard was the sweep of the wind, bringing with it new snow.

One day, just as his fire was about to die, a strong young man came to his lodge. The young man's face was red with youth, and his eyes twinkled with life. His lips formed a warm smile. His walk was gentle and light, and on his head he wore a wreath of grass in place of a warrior's band. In his hands he carried no bow and arrow, but instead, a bunch of flowers.

The old man spoke first. "My son," he said, "I am glad to see you. Come in. Come tell me of your adventures and journeys. Let us talk the night away. I will tell you of my experience, and of what I can do. You will tell me the same, and we will entertain each other."

As the young man entered, the old man brought out of his sack an old pipe, and filled it with tobacco. He handed it to his young guest, and together they smoked. When the ceremony was over, they took turns speaking of their powers.

"I breathe," began the old man, "and the waters still. Streams and lakes become stiff and hard, like clear stones."

"I blow my breath," said the young man, "and flowers appear all over the land."

The old man was challenged, so he spoke again. "I shake my hair," he said, "and snow covers the land. Leaves fall. Flowers hide, or my breath blows them all away. Birds fly to far away lands. Animals run to caves and holes. The ground itself becomes as hard as flint."

"I shake my locks," the young man said confidently, "and warm showers fall upon the land. Plants lift their heads up out of the ground, and birds come to my voice. The warmth in my breath unlocks the waters, and music plays where I walk. Nature celebrates."

They spoke all night. At length, the sun began to rise. The lodge and its surrounding land began to warm.

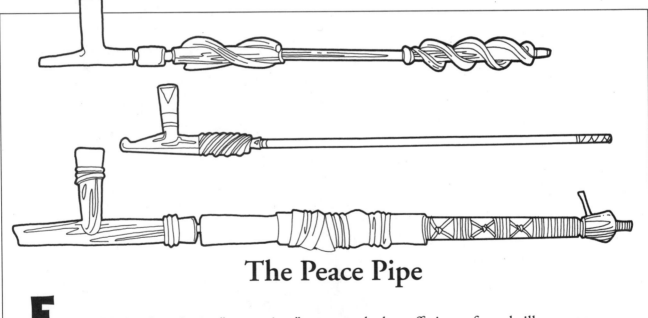

The Peace Pipe

For most Native Americans, "peace pipes" were smoked as offerings of goodwill to guests and friends, as offerings to the spirits, and as cures for diseases. In some ceremonies, the smoker blew in all four directions for health and good luck.

The way a pipe was held was important. Holding it incorrectly was bad luck, and dropping it could even mean death.

The old man's tongue stopped. He heard a robin and a bluebird singing sweetly atop the lodge. By the door, the stream began to trickle. The softly moving wind brought with it not snow, but the sweet smell of flowers and herbs.

As the sun rose, the young man realized that his host was Winter itself—and as the world around him warmed, the old man's eyes began to stream tears. His time was ending.

The sun heated the land, and the old man began to shrink. Soon he had melted completely away. All that remained in his spot was a tiny white flower—the first flower of the spring.

The young man breathed deeply, and listened to the world awaken.

THE MAN WHO WISHED FOR ETERNAL LIFE

A Menomini Story

Once, there was a great hero of the Menomini people. His name was Manabush. People took his advice often, and they relied upon him a great deal. But eventually, like many great heroes, Manabush went away from his people to live alone.

Long after this great hero had left his people, there was a time of starvation among the Menomini. The hunting was very bad, and winter was coming. If something did not happen soon, people would begin to die.

One night, an Indian dreamed that Manabush spoke to him. But the Indian could not understand what Manabush said in the dream. When the Indian woke up, he went to the chiefs of the nation for counsel.

"What does this dream mean?" he asked.

The chiefs thought hard. After much talk, one of them said, "The dream is telling us that Manabush can help our people. We must seek him and ask for what we want."

The dreamer blackened his face in preparation for the journey. Then he rejoined the chiefs and they set off to search for Manabush.

After a long hike, they came to the shore of the Great Waters, where they got into canoes. It was a hard journey. They paddled for a long, long time in their trip across the water, until they reached a jagged, rocky shore in the Land of the Rising Sun, where Manabush dwelled.

At last, they came to a tipi.

"Hello?" they called. "Is anyone there?"

Manabush saw who was outside, and invited them to come in. The door of the tipi lifted and fell as each one entered and sat down. Manabush was glad to see them.

"My friends," he said, "why is it you come to visit me? It is a long and hard journey to get here. What do you wish?"

All at once, the chiefs responded, "Manabush, we have come to you for help. We need good medicine for hunting, so that we may supply our people with food."

"You will have it," said Manabush. Then he turned to the silent Indian. "What is it you wish?" he said.

"I do not want hunting medicine," the dreamer replied. "I want to live forever."

Manabush wrinkled his brow, and rose. He walked slowly toward the Indian.

"Nothing is everlasting," he said. "Everything must go one day." But the Indian would not hear it.

"You are powerful, Manabush," said the Indian. "Please help me become eternal."

Manabush was not happy. "As you wish," he grunted. At that moment, the Indian turned into a smooth, gray rock.

"You will be a stone, for it is only a stone that is everlasting," he proclaimed. With that, the chiefs rose and left the tipi to return to their own land.

Everyone had received his wish.

THE HERO TWINS AND THE GIANT

A Tewa Story

The Sun had twin boys, Maw-Sahv and Oo-yah-wee. Their mother was a Tewa. They were known as the Hero Twins, and they had special strengths.

When the twins were born, they grew strong almost instantly, and as soon as they were a minute old, they began to play on the desert.

The twins grew up very quickly, and they had some amazing adventures while they were still very young. When other boys their age were still toddlers, the Hero Twins had become famous hunters and fearsome warriors.

Still, they were boys. They loved to play pranks, and they loved to hear tales of adventure. Luckily for them, their grandmother loved to tell stories. One of their favorites was a series of stories she told them about a giantess who lived deep inside a mountain to the south. She was gruesome, and she was the terror of the land. These stories frightened the boys a bit, but they longed to encounter this wondrous, frightful beast.

One day, while their grandmother was busy, Maw-Sahv and Oo-yah-wee stole away from home. Bows and arrows on their backs, they walked for miles and miles, until they reached a great forest. It lay at the foot of a huge mountain.

There, right in front of them, at the edge of the forest, was the Giant-woman. She sat leaning against a tall tree—it was tall to the twins, but just right for her—and slept heavily in the sun.

The Giant-woman was much more frightening than the boys had imagined. She was bigger and uglier, too. The twins could not move. They were frozen in fear.

Maw-Sahv signaled Oo-yah-wee to back away slowly from the forest, and to quietly steal home. They began their retreat.

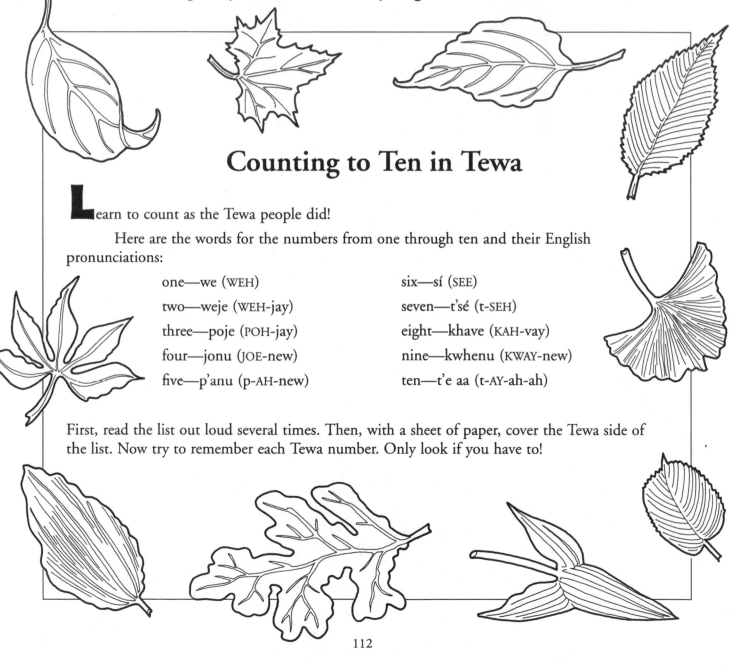

Counting to Ten in Tewa

Learn to count as the Tewa people did!

Here are the words for the numbers from one through ten and their English pronunciations:

one—we (WEH)   six—sí (SEE)
two—weje (WEH-jay)   seven—t'sé (t-SEH)
three—poje (POH-jay)   eight—khave (KAH-vay)
four—jonu (JOE-new)   nine—kwhenu (KWAY-new)
five—p'anu (p-AH-new)   ten—t'e aa (t-AY-ah-ah)

First, read the list out loud several times. Then, with a sheet of paper, cover the Tewa side of the list. Now try to remember each Tewa number. Only look if you have to!

Just then, the Giant-woman stirred. Her eyes were not open, but she lifted her head and sniffed deeply—something smelled good. She opened her eyes.

Then she saw the twins. She smiled a cracked, rotten smile. "Come here, boys," she said. "Come and get into this basket of mine, and I will take you to my house for dinner."

Oo-yah-wee didn't know what to do. But Maw-Sahv had a plan. "Very well," he said. "If you take us through the forest, we will join you at your home for dinner."

The Giant-woman smiled an ugly smile, for she did not mean that the boys would join her for dinner—she meant that she would eat them. But she promised to take them through the forest before they went to her home.

The twins climbed into her basket, which was large enough for ten boys, and they started off into the forest. As she carried them through the woods, they playfully grabbed at the branches of pine trees. When one of them broke off in Maw-Sahv's hands and sap began to run from the end of the branch, Maw-Sahv had a thought.

"I know how we can escape," he whispered to his brother.

"What was that?" grunted the Giant-woman.

"Uhh—I said, 'You have a lovely cape,'" Maw-Sahv responded quickly. Oo-yah-wee breathed a sigh of relief.

"Thank you," said the giant. "Now keep quiet!"

They did. But they also broke off more pine branches, and collected the sap in their hands. Then, carefully, they rubbed the sap on the giant's head and back. Without noticing, the Giant-woman sat down to rest.

While they were on the ground, the twins hopped out of the basket, collected the largest stones they could find, and loaded the basket with stones. Then they set fire to Giant-woman's hair, and scrambled up a nearby tree to hide.

The Giant-woman did not notice that her hair was on fire. The fire burnt slowly on top of her head—sap takes a moment to get going. She got up and lifted the basket. She did not notice that the boys were gone—the basket felt as heavy as before. She walked on, thinking how good the plump boys were going to taste. For a moment, she even thought that she could smell them cooking.

After a few minutes, the Giant-woman's head and cape were ablaze. She howled in pain, a great howl that shook the trees, and she dropped her basket.

"AAAAAAAAAAAAAAAAAAhhhhhhrgh!" she screamed, rolling on the ground to put out the flame. But it would not go out right away—to stop the fire, she had to grind her head on the ground like a grain pestle.

Snorting in anger, the Giant-woman got up. Her head was sore and badly scorched. She went to collect her basket, and became even angrier when she found cold, hard rocks instead of the juicy twins. Carefully, she retraced her steps.

Back where she had rested, the boys were lying unconscious on the ground—her scream had shaken them out of the tree, and their fall had knocked them out.

"Come along, you naughty children," she said as she lifted their limp bodies into the basket again. "We are almost home."

Soon they reached her home, deep in the side of a mountain. She set the boys down, and stretched her long arms wide—they ached from the journey.

"Boys, go to the back of the house, where I keep the firewood. Bring me a lot of wood, so that I can bake you a sweet cake."

Knowing that they couldn't escape, they did as she said. With the wood, the Giant-woman built a roaring fire in the adobe oven just outside her house.

"Now go wash up for dinner, boys," she said to them. "I don't want my food to be dirty—I mean, I don't want you to eat food when you're dirty."

The boys washed up well, and when their backs were turned to her, the Giant-woman grabbed them by the necks. With a great laugh, she threw them into the oven and covered the door with a huge slab of rock.

Try as they might, the twins could not budge the rock.

But as fate would have it, a group of spirit friends of the Hero Twins, the Trues, were watching. They did not let the fire harm the boys, and when the Giant-woman had gone back inside her house, the Trues helped the boys escape through the smoke hole on top of the oven.

Next the twins caught hundreds of snakes and toads in the nearby forest, and dropped them into the oven through the smoke hole. Then they hid behind a large rock to watch.

The next day, the Giant-woman stepped outside and yawned. She walked over to the oven and sniffed.

"Whooh!" she said, holding her nose. "Those twins don't smell very good."

The boys laughed behind the rock, and the Giant-woman looked in their direction. She saw a flock of birds fly from a nearby tree, and decided that was the sound she had heard.

Inside the house, the Giant-woman's baby daughter began to cry. Clearly, the Giant-baby was hungry.

"We will eat soon," she yelled. And she unsealed the oven. Smoke poured out.

The Giant-woman put the odd-looking mess of meat on a large platter and took it inside.

They have cooked away into almost nothing, she thought, *but they will taste good just the same.*

She and the baby sat down to eat, and devoured the disgusting meal. The Hero Twins laughed all through her breakfast, but the Giant-woman was chewing so loudly that she could not hear them. Suddenly, the Giant-woman began to choke. She turned green—then blue—then purple—and fell dead. The Giant-baby did the same.

The boys could not tell what had happened. Carefully, they crept up to the house to see.

"She has eaten a poisonous toad," they exclaimed, dancing with joy. They were free to go home!

But, being the curious boys that they were, they decided to explore inside the mountain before they left. Taking bows and arrows, they set off into the deep caverns behind the Giant-woman's home in search of more adventure.

But that is another tale.

HOW THE HERO TWINS OUTWITTED THE STORM KING

A Tewa Story

No one loved adventure more than the Hero Twins. After they had conquered the most terrible monster in the land, the fearsome Giant-woman, they could have set off straight for home and enjoyed a feast of praise and celebration. Instead, the two boys decided to go exploring.

Behind the Giant-woman's home at the base of the mountain were deep caverns. These caverns were damp, and musty, and very dark. The twins boldly stepped inside and began their way down a passage.

For a long time, the only sound they heard was the echo of their own footsteps. But suddenly, a great rumbling came from further back inside the mountain. On they went.

The boys were quite hungry. They were just about to turn back for food when they saw light coming from around a bend in the cave.

The twins ran to it. It was a huge room, and it was filled with vegetables! There were melons, and pumpkins, and corn—enough food for a lifetime! But they could not see how it grew.

After a tasty meal, the boys decided to continue their exploration. They could see that the light in the room was coming

from another room beyond. The light streamed out so brightly that it seemed as if a small sun had decided to rest within the caves.

As they went on, the rumbling they had heard before came again—but this time much louder. It seemed to come from the same place as the light.

Finally, they came to a room of solid rock, a room so bright and loud that they had to shut their eyes and cover their ears. Squinting, Maw-Sahv and Oo-yah-wee looked around.

All along the walls were large spears of shimmering light that shook ever so often. This was where the rumbling came from! Oo-yah-wee picked up a spear, and held it.

"What is this, brother?" he asked, tossing it to Maw-Sahv.

The spear shot through the air so fast that Maw-Sahv could not catch it—he jumped out of the way just in time to avoid being hit. The spear crashed into the ground with a huge flash and an incredible, "BOOM!"

"I believe we have found lightning," said Maw-Sahv, brushing himself off. "We should head home."

And they did—but not without taking a few spears with them.

When the boys reached their home, they told their grandmother of their adventures. She held her face in amazement, but she had a hard time believing them. It was only when they took out the spears of lightning and began tossing them around that she fully understood.

Their thunder rumbled throughout the pueblo, and people ran inside, thinking a storm was coming. The Hero Twins just laughed, and tossed their spears. They had taken the blue lightning of the West, the yellow lightning of the North, the red lightning of the East, and the white lightning of the South—and they played with all of it

happily, not caring what others thought. They did not worry about who owned the lightning.

Just about that time, the storm king, Shee-wo-nah, entered the thunder-room inside the mountain. He wanted to make a great storm, and when he noticed that some of the lightning was missing he shook with anger, causing a rumble to be heard across the world.

The Hero Twins were busy playing with the lightning outside, and when they heard the rumble they stopped for a moment.

"Did we do that?" Maw-Sahv asked his twin.

"We must have," said Oo-yah-wee, and they continued to play.

In a rage, Shee-wo-nah flew through the sky on a thundercloud to the pueblo where the twins lived. When they saw him coming, the Hero Twins ran inside their house and locked the door. The storm king landed with a loud thud.

He pounded on the door.

"You have taken my lightning!" he bellowed. "Return it, and no harm will come to your village."

But the boys, like many boys, did not know when to stop. "Make us!" they yelled back, and made faces at the storm king through the door.

The storm king did intend to make them return the lightning. He summoned a huge thunderstorm, the largest he had ever called. Rain poured down like a great waterfall. Lightning slammed into the ground. Thunder boomed like a thousand drums.

But the boys would not obey. Inside the house, they rattled the lightning spears and made thunder of their own.

The storm king was furious. He made the rain fall even harder. Water poured in through the chimney of the twins' house and began to fill up the rooms.

"We will drown!" cried Maw-Sahv.

"Make it stop!" Oo-yah-wee begged the storm king. But now it was the storm king's turn to laugh. And he laughed loudly.

The Trues were watching again nearby, and they wanted to help the Hero Twins. They knew that the twins were still boys, and that one day, when they had grown up, they would do great things for their people. So they sent Badger to help.

Badger dug a tunnel from outside the house up through the floor of the twins' home. The water began to rush out, and with it came the twins—and the spears of lightning.

Riding the current of this new river, the twins escaped with the lightning, and when the storm king finally broke inside their house, he found it empty. He rumbled in anger, but it was no use.

The Hero Twins had outwitted the storm king, and they lived a long, happy life full of many more adventures.